OUR ANIMAL

OUR ANIMAL

MEREDITH STRICKER

OMNIDAWN PUBLISHING

OAKLAND, CALIFORNIA

2016

Cover art © Canan Tolon
Untitled, 1996; acrylic, oil and rust on linen; 76 X 61 cm / 30 X 24 inches

Photo of Franz Kafka on page 53 © HIP / Art Resource, NY
Franz Kafka (1883-1924), Czech writer, as a university student, 1913.
Jewish Chronicle Archive

Cover and interior design by Gillian Olivia Blythe Hamel

Offset printed in the United States
by Edwards Brothers Malloy, Ann Arbor, Michigan
On 55# Heritage Book Cream White Antique

Library of Congress Cataloging-in-Publication Data

Names: Stricker, Meredith, author.
Title: Our animal / Meredith Stricker.
Description: Oakland, California : Omnidawn Publishing, 2016.
Identifiers: LCCN 2015040780 | ISBN 9781632430199 (pbk. : alk. paper)
Classification: LCC PS3619.T747 A6 2016 | DDC 811/.6--dc23
LC record available at http://lccn.loc.gov/2015040780

Published by Omnidawn Publishing, Oakland, California
www.omnidawn.com (510) 237-5472 (800) 792-4957
10 9 8 7 6 5 4 3 2 1
ISBN: 978-1-63243-019-9

for my mother, who was an interpreter at the Nuremberg Trials

and in memory of my father, illuminating physician

Now that we are post-modern—although who knows, perhaps we're post-post-modern—and understand just how slippery language can be, is it possible to agree on any absolute "truth"? Keats's ouroboros definition, truth equals beauty equals truth, seems uselessly naïve as soon as we admit that the idea of beauty is culturally determined and often self-servingly imposed from above by those with wealth and power. Even if we did believe in an inalienable truth, where might we look for it? In poetic lines? The pages of a diary? Interwoven with the plot of a novel? Below the cold surface of a boilerplate statement of policy handed out to company employees? In final thoughts written on slips of paper preserved against a dying writer's wishes? All of these? Some? None?

Another, more technical, question is whether disjunction and collage are better than linearity at approaching any residual notion of truth in a rapidly changing world? Franz Kafka died on 3 June 1924, three years before Walter Benjamin first mentioned his collage project, *Passagenwerk*, in a letter to a friend, two years after Eliot published *The Waste Land*, almost ten years after Pound began his *Cantos*, twelve years after Stein began writing *Tender Buttons*. While not formally collagist, might Kafka's combined production, much of written as fragments that were later selectively glued together by Max Brod, be thought of as a collage? How does one begin to represent any of these writers and their work when their lives and what they wrote continually spiral around the axis of the industrial revolution, Freudian psychology, Emile Durkheim's normless anomie, political dissolution, and the multifarious death machine of World War I? If one looks back at the body of turn-of-the-century literature, the instability of that moment appears to have produced brainwave oscillations that resulted in a new way of writing about the timeless problem of being human and, yes, animal.

Today's lyric poets have inherited the Modernist question of how to make sense of great complexity, as well as the question of what we should call what we are looking for, now that the concept of "truth" looks like a tired, untrustworthy, abstract ideal. To that end, Meredith Stricker has taken bits of Kafka's writing, disembodied those bits, and wedded them (welded them) to her own pressing lyric meditations. The result is an intricate collage that feels like a machine fabric that's been taken apart, thread by thread, and then rewoven by hand. The form seems apt as a way to represent the present, which if anything is more inscrutably elaborate, and certainly as disordered if not more so, than Kafka's era. As Stricker writes in her Whitmanesque-Ginsbergian, push-of-speech preface-poem, "Why Not in the Forest | preface," there is still something to search for:

> … if not solace,
>
> kinship, if not kinship, a flash of alienation
>
> in abeyance, breathing space between
>
> grassblades and grassblades shivering in a field, light passing
>
> rapidly through broken clouds, rent by a raw disconsolate edge
>
> of *cigáne* music, the beatings, oxen tethered and worn into
>
> bones, frail smoky flame, the sharp wind's cinders and
>
> blackened throat, anomie, anomaly gone asunder and now
>
> the sudden éclat of sparks and thunder of trains laden with dark
>
> quarried basalt alongside rabbits who scatter on track's edge
>
> and our not knowing if the moment of being
>
> discovered and devoured has arrived
>
> > in snowfall, no trace later

These poems feel like actual physical traces of the experience of reading Kafka, where pieces of text now inhabit the cellular structure of Stricker's brain. And which she in turn imprints on our brains. Kafka's "then" and "I" have been married to Stricker's "I" and "now." The groom dared to be, to write, and to die. The bride dares to marry the groom's daring. She is existing, writing, and dying within his afterimage. Beneath the rhetorical surface, the marriage and textual melding, are such questions as: who speaks to us, and who speaks when we speak? The answer—". . . tossed on currents of Revolution, World Wars, treaties, forged and betrayed, flotsam of humanity, a single glossolaic crow feather buoyant on the spars and tumults of fathomless flood-swollen rivers"—is that we are who we are *and* who we read: one composite animal that is inevitably other.

The continual back and forth movement of this multi-layered, multi-sourced story of literary kinship over time comes to resemble the pacing of a caged bear. The *va-et-vient* takes place between Stricker and Kafka, as well as between the two them and us, the readers, animals all. As they pace within the enclosure-like poems, the border between what Kafka wrote and what Stricker is writing disolves, and as it does, unattributed fragments rise to the surface out of what appears to be the static of the two talking over one another: "That's o.k. I show up later anyway" "a stray dog scuffles behind a dumpster" "wants earth" "like a blond wax" "angel Madonna doll." There are even flashes here and there of what might be taken for truth. Not the old idea of truth, a polished-to-perfection gem, but a Janus-faced truth that resists the falsity of sound-bite reductive purity and edges closer instead to the convulsive beauty of surrealism. In the chaos of any given moment, on the mirror at the back of the cage we can see ourselves looking first here, then there—"I" "a" "wax" "doll"—as we mime Stricker's search for some consoling likeness.

—Mary Jo Bang,
judge of the Omnidawn Open Poetry Book Prize

CONTENTS

WHY NOT IN THE FOREST | preface

"I have never been here before; my breath comes differently,
the sun is outshone by the star beside it." Kafka *[Zürau No 17]*

where each reading renders a new book, one that has never

existed before and we are its pages and its pages have cast us

forth as tough mongrel sema until something bruised, wounded

and untouchable finds solace if not solace,

history,

kinship, if not kinship, a flash of alienation

an unwritten letter

in abeyance, breathing space between

grassblades and grassblades shivering in a field, light passing

rapidly through broken clouds, rent by a raw disconsolate edge

of *cigáne* music, the beatings, oxen tethered and worn into

bones, frail smoky flame, the sharp wind's cinders and

blackened throat, anomie, anomaly gone asunder and now

the sudden éclat of sparks and thunder of trains laden with dark

quarried basalt alongside rabbits who scatter on track's edge

and our not knowing if the moment of being

discovered and devoured has arrived

in snowfall, no trace later

there is a wilderness between cells, between us, the longing

of words chained to the specificity of syntax which they slip

past in the night — *"why not in the forest, where the air moves freely?"*

amniotic

anamnesis

our mineral

complicity

MATERIALS: poems printed randomly and accidentally over the wrong side of previous drafts used as scratch-paper, *"conversation slips"* Kafka wrote as he lay dying of tuberculosis of the throat unable to speak at a clinic in Kierling, scraps from his *Zürau Aphorisms*, *Blue Octavo Notebooks* and diaries

OUR ANIMAL

CHAPTER ONE: HEAVEN

when Kafka said "I'm a cage in search of a bird",
he was speaking the language of birds, crow-black
in heaven, revolving like a planet, he sways on
wires with such great care watching us lose our
way — *"we were created to live in Paradise, and
Paradise was designed to serve us. Our destination has
been changed; we are not told whether this has
happened to Paradise as well." [Zürau No 84]*

a landscape of glass in shattered heaps – the bird-
fountained *pardes* of fig and pomegranate groves
where a drop of water's horrific transparency
floods the parched throat of ashy photographs
whose anonymous inhabitants lock their gaze
upon ours – remembrance everywhere thickened
and rushing like a fever, an embrace for which

sensation remains but no names in a vivid amnesia
we call the present arriving in remnants to
scavenge as after the war and imprisonment by
successive opposing regimes when Géza half-
starved and working as an itinerant pianist while

raw
testmony

he was house-sitting the chic apartment
of Porsche's mistress and devouring the
sausage ration destined for the mistress's
schnauzer – "but Butzi's looking so *thin*", "yes of
course, I've been taking him for long walks on
the *Königstrasse*" as it's dawning on us that even if
we somehow ferreted out our destination there
would be no maps

into microphones
simultaneous

veer or error toward
paradise
covered in amber
dark-winged slits
a white moth,
then abyss

CHAPTER TWO: GOD

god

snowfields everywhere out to the horizon
clotted mud and snow   thick as a mind losing its reason
god is hunger in leaves the sound I hear

losing all trace   of light
in a drop of blood
and gravity,   a mind threshed, flattened
a god who doesn't is one I can believe in

neither of us has papers or fixed abode
knotted   the color blue falls down
buckles   like a shot bird
where I don't exist

my heart is   cold as the horizon
and I am told I will
and I have lost   everything   burr, bone
place

they used to sing
this infinite   random   wounded
now I hear them all
sense of touch   this horizon

not singing god   change into an animal
forest of my   brain undone——

23

straining toward gentility, the drawing room's awkward furniture dulled and staring, figurines and embroidery, endless embroidery, the dark carved sideboard with its unloved soup tureen amidst conversation like pruned hedges, going nowhere, hemmed in stitch by stitch, white linen turned grayish and unappetizing pressed raw after countless washings, the stealthy pulse of a mantle clock is the most alive thing in unaired, curtained rooms

                    seemed to gather

    smoke

                              the underworld's

antennae

        "real life"

                            hissing

CHAPTER THREE: ELSEWHERE

for thirty kreuzers

trembling

swollen, unholy, scrubby

strange as

"the delicate throat of a girl"

seen once

CHAPTER FOUR: A G-D [OR AN INSEKT] WHO DOESN'T EXIST IS ONE I CAN BELIEVE IN

the color blue falls down yes, it's wounded, people are changing into animals and back again or used to but what Transliteration of species to species to mythos would suit the New Man of office cubicles and triplicate forms? the color blue approaches, falls down, was once heaven now litter pushed sodden into gutters – Gregor *could* "buckle like a shot bird" but that would be presuming on the plummet of a wild creature strapped pellet-torn and gaping onto Franz-Josef's gamekeeper's belt, it would be like gate-crashing the exam questions brought on a silver platter by attendants wearing white gloves at the no-Jews

Gymnasium facing rows of Herr-Doctor-Professor statuary, the Committee of cleverly masked brutality taking afternoon schnapps — it has been brought to our attention that neither G–d nor Gregor's newly revealed self has papers or fixed abode, therefore they are knotted into a hybrid Beast — mechanical and pistoned with insect legs, the feathered gods used to sing with human desire, the woodcock, the wild onion fronds and swans but now they fall on their backs squeaking and rock helplessly inarticulate as defective metal plates in a linotype machine

                                                    monotheistic

adamantine

                insomnia   chalky

                                            as typhus

while in the clotted mud and snow that was
wartime, conflagration that was once a god,
hunger in leaves, sound heard in a drop of blood,
we are no longer suitable to becoming animals,
not yet sufficiently re-radicalized but a *transition-
animal*, an *Insekt*, yes, perhaps this might be
possible – he has been such a one – mind threshed,
flattened, knotted, anaerobic

where cerulean blue falls down and awakens
as an Indeterminate-insect-being

awakens as an untranslatable word

CHAPTER FIVE: THE UNWANTED

heaven of underneath

heaven of untraceable

heaven of cold stones

heaven of the unseen

heaven of uncounted

heaven of lost animals

heaven of accident

heaven of falling

heaven of make-shift

heaven of tramways

heaven of haberdashery

heaven of salesmen on commission

heaven of left-overs

heaven of triplicate forms

heaven of trash-bins

heaven of expired coupons

heaven of mended cloth

heaven of unraveled seams

heaven of shoes

heaven of wrongful termination

heaven of waiting rooms

heaven of subsidiary rights

heaven of a lighted match

finding oneself a repulsive insect

in an orderly, uncomprehending

home and then pelted

by an enraged, boorish Father

with lethally inflicted apples from

the kitsch rococo fruit bowl

on the sideboard – to be born

an Outsider knowing how

the antennae of the unwanted

and exterminated feel

then how far Understanding

can move   – into crevices,

unstinting

little crumbs of crushed para-

dise

                            wide-screen

        demilitarized zone

                                      every hair on his body

wildlife now traverses freely

CHAPTER SIX: FALLING UPRIGHT

"a cage went in search of a bird" [Kafka, Zürau No 16]

"form shaped by the mobile,

the moving, the liquid…"

sift swift cast into air like wheat

we are falling upright, are falling standing still

"certain images and phrases are repeated but in other contexts"

continually rewrite themselves, it would seem, endlessly

the way his yellowish hair slipped down in back from the bald spot

it was supposed to cover like bird feathers

what appears

being "made" into a "poem"

CHAPTER SEVEN: SWOON

"Not until twilight did Gregor awake out of a deep sleep, more like a swoon than a sleep ... The electric lights in the street cast a pale sheen here and there on the ceiling and the upper surfaces of the furniture. His legs on one side fluttered trembling in the air..."

a roaring in the ears like traffic and waterfalls clamor, clammy the skin feels like someone else's, is someone else's — the punch-line untranslatable as one of Löwy's ludicrous sketches at the *Bar Kochba*, the one about a guy and a cockroach — later he says *"in Hebrew my name is Amschel"* after his grandfather who bathed in the river everyday even if he had to chop through winter ice and his skin ached red and stubborn in the cold

ecstatic   fuel rods

a fly lands

tunneling into words

how many names will he accumulate before he dies? it may be possible for him to be everyone else since it is clearly out of the question to locate himself in a fixed *identitas* being more suited to taking on the character of a pebble, cracked and gray, found near the *Karlúv* bridge or that of a chipped plate, a sparrow with spindly legs – everywhere he looks is a mirror and nothing reflected recognizable as himself except this stranger with "luminous eyes" whose gaze seems startlingly alive – *"perhaps only because I was just then observing myself and wanted to frighten myself"*

an unhieratic

mammal

brainstem

/ storm

CHAPTER EIGHT: ANOTHER SKY

the body has melted, swallows dip their wings

CHAPTER NINE: COMMERCE

"how many years will you be able to stand it? …
how long will I be able to stand your standing it?"

to be dying not really very old, after all – just 40, still
unmarried, skilled in confinement, a life spent in
offices like the Assicuranzioni Generale Insurance
Company of Prague where *no employee has the right to*
keep any other objects than those belonging to the Office
under lock in the desk and files assigned for his use – a good
place to practice suffering or the acute, unmediated
observation accorded by suffering alongside tedious
accounts of dust – o burn us into miniscule flakes,
flecks of God caught like spinach between the teeth,
at lunch-break bored pigeons scuffle over kabalistic
redemption sparks and you imagine the swift
exploded light of a *"beautiful hour, masterful state, garden*
gone wild, you turn from the house and see rushing toward
you on the garden path the goddess of happiness"

                  oasis of
         undressed   millennia
gone

                                 green-gold in the light

Usually people forget me. They listen to him

8:00 am, Johannesburg Exchange, interest rates, hedge funds, polar icecap
about me, but really they're seeing themselves.

11:00 am, Kuwait Exchange
I don't speak—a silence embedded in the spines of cactus

2:00 pm, Singapore Exchange, tonight's new moon leaves skies dark
at least not in his bearing. Also a lot of light pours
around me Angels, etcetera. Hummingbirds veer off course

3:00 pm, Rio Exchange, a stray dog scuffles behind a dumpster
blinded and crash into the glass partition

2:00 pm, Shanghai Exchange, limits and
they go out once, limits and say you... a weed wants earth

1:00 pm, Chicago Exchange
probably already forgotten about me sharp

4:00 pm, Sydney Exchange, time's festivs everywhere
That's o.k. I show up later anyway

Existence is netted and complex, everything's talking

9:00 am, Amman Exchange, flight of birds startles a street-cleaner
at once even molecules chant and sway, speak in tongues

in this instant, time may be global but each moment local, unrepeatable
phosphor-luminescent polypeptide chains.

in this instant, a family
Existence dresses

in words so we can get excited about it

in this instant, sudden wings, wash of light, things that happen
For instance, the word Memory

footstep on land, and those we love
interests me a lot. Intersects. I'll start over.

in this instant, I have a ticket for redemption, no market-share
Remembering can never bring back

in sparrows unfreshing tail wags
the beloved. What it brings back is not what was

But now is. It burns us up into miniscule flakes

fourteen kinds of grey in an ordinary sky.
Something new. Something new is remembered, is

flying home, a hawk's wings
I have to admit most of the time it was awful

blurring in close at wind
having him close at hand like that. He was awkward and

no stock-options
his eyes were heavy on me. I felt like a sparrow in a thicket

held in. But at least he was, well, interested

in an overpass shelter whose freeway roar
And, except for his wife, faithful. But to what? It wasn't me

reveals another kind of rapture
he saw. It wasn't me he built in memory, like a blond wax

weedy outside. angel Madonna doll. He forgot to see me when he remembered

This is what is called love
of commerce

CHAPTER TEN: HUNGER

unable to eat because of the tuberculosis spread to his throat,

he is starving to death in the clinic as proofs for *A Hunger Artist* arrive

"Here, now, with what strength I have am I to write it" —

and what was the secret of the Hunger Artist who astonished so many?

"I couldn't find anything I wanted to eat"

yes it is true, the soul is a crow, the soul shines with reflected sky

coal wings bright wings diving and scuttling in the wildest winds

not at all who you expected to show up

                            cortex

                                      bitten

                                                taxes

waving their arms   resume drilling

                                      @Bayreuth

broken branches
attending, ascending, we go down deep
shadow becomes forest

Here are some ways the Soul has shown up
the trees are human

Swimmers in the Hudson, singular in their swarming, dark, threshing the water
people are animal-woods with leaves

arms flail sign language signaling inexplicable presence, I am here
in the selves of their shining cells

"my name writ in water", jellyfish, many varieties, especially those
the smallest

"small" and "speckled" as Dickinson inventories in her taxonomy of soul species
and largest particles

Their ability to take the form of their surroundings, the luminosity
vibrating stars

and phosphorescence, their sting, the crystalline forms of diatoms in Haeckel's
tremulous

illustrations like microscopic transistor radio parts mixed with jewelry
on your eyelid

geodes , hallucinogenically precise flowers, a road sign at night on an empty
in black

highway, twisted purple flamed figures from Rodin's Gates of Hell, as unlike
sunlight

Hellenic marbles as possible, off-kilter, swaying, the body of a woman

CHAPTER ELEVEN: CROWS

anaphoric
animation

not much in our story will make sense
unless you know that the word for crow in
Czech is the superbly onomatopoetic
"kavka" and Kafka's father used the crow
as an emblem for his business and you may
have noticed crows continually kav-ka-ing
in various degrees of hoarseness across
pine canyons as these pages form and the
sounds of entreaty rattle in their throats
and though they are larger than other birds
and can chase hawks from their territory
fearlessly they are also quite shy and
awkward on branches, their tenderness
apparent as they groom each other for
feather-lice patiently in the rain, their raw
uncouth language meeting our ears with
incomprehension

in a violent rainstorm

head-first, shining

unmet,

unbuyable

Immaculate animalcule

CHAPTER TWELVE: FATHER

it's surprising it's taken us this long to come to the Father Chapter since all chapters could have in some way been titled Father or God or the Overthrow of One or the Other or forms of Subjugation by either or both – here's Father Crow with his huge head, raucous cries and ungainly manners who says "dear son, let us go to the beer garden in the park, let us eat sausages in the company of men while I deflect my own awkwardness and embarrassment by humiliating you for your frail, white body in the beer garden at the Civilian Swimming School" – this, of course, is nothing like what Kafka's father said to him, except the part about sausages, since it was arranged that all self-awareness was left to the son who was merciless in seeing through appearance

"How we used to undress, for example, in the little dark
cabin; how he would then drag me out, because I was
ashamed; how he tried then to teach me the little bit of
swimming he pretended to know ... Then we used to sit
together naked at the buffet each with a sausage and a
pint of beer ... Just try to imagine the picture properly —
this enormous man, holding a little nervous bag of bones
by the hand" — this Titan Cronos, *Son-Eater* with an
immense Stein of lager in his hands though it now
appears Immortality has other plans

/pitchblende

"poplar whirled out of the earth by a tornado"

restless

CHAPTER THIRTEEN: ELECTRON-DENSITY CLOUD

"A faith like an axe. As heavy, as light"   *Zürau No 87*

and we are left with his inferno as tiny video game circles

of hell of earth of paradise of birth

and death and in-between   where each day we get out of bed
blue impossibility refraction
                    matter now understood as "likelihood"
            to redeem the beauty of every sentient

                          unfurls in a quantum floral
        being, rock, tongue   "of being found at a given place at a given time"
            because of the

                narrow passage-way
            grain of salt

                        a threaded needle, across a chasm
                shaped, astrological petaling

                you traverse a land where dinosaurs once walked, the sun
            resembles
                                bright on your face
                        pores of the skin

        electron density cloud
                smell of gasoline and trucks
                        Dante's harrowed rose Paradiso

            space and time

                    fiore, mind flower

CHAPTER FOURTEEN: TREE OF LIFE

our expulsion from paradise is most apparent in ordinary things made banal by repetition, indifference and insomnia, all he can do is shudder and grow weary of the lack of Archangels and turn to the clamor of past gods whose fates entwine with thunder and swans, who speak as willows or fast-moving streams emergent from the clatter of dishes and trams

their chaste

instrument

December 8: *"Bed, constipation, pain in the back, irritable evening, cat in the room, dissension"*, yesterday there was pig-sticking, later he sees all Life Pythagorically as a simplified recalculation expressed outside the con-tamination of any codified *religio-*, that is, that there are three things: *"looking at oneself as something alien, forgetting the sight, remembering the gaze"* actually, it can be boiled down to two points — *"for the third includes the second."*

not graves / *die graben*

— seed-fields

harrowed

fur

CHAPTER FIFTEEN: RUST

a record of his days could be mapped like blockages
on a doctor's x-ray or a traffic controller's
nightmare – each road, every turn seems thwarted
or occluded by unexpected even ridiculous forces:
weather, inertia, accident, absurd altercations
"December 22 Lumbago, mental arithmetic at night"
"January 17 Walk to Oberlau. Limitations"   the corolla
"January 22 Attempt to walk to Michlob. Mud"   of strangeness
he wonders what can he possibly have to do with
Greatness and considers something his friend Stein
said the other day: *the Bible is sanctum, the World*
sputum – and thus the difficulty of inhabiting his
own thoughts which race ahead snuffling the air
more ardently than a pack of hounds so that he feels
he must give up any illusion of controlling one's
destiny, to become accustomed to living the life of a
splinter in an athlete's torso, an inflammation
antithetical to history's glories and progress,
corrosive rust on medals and speeches

       what connects   phosphorescence

          plankton, iron ore

    a memory of which he had no memory

CURRICULUM VITAE

SIMULTANEOUS FIELD-WIKIS
have you noticed how

IMMEDIATE WITH EVERY PARTICLE
a deconstructed self still demands

OF HISTORY, CRUSHED SEED-POD
tenure

SUFFUSED WITH GEOLOGIC TIME
hard to part from the beloved

AND STARS LIVING OR DEAD
holy vitae

"selvaggio è aspro e fort   to become clear

as a glass of water

Wild and rough and stubborn, my Dante exiled
my soul doesn't know

on itinerant paths with briars, a dead poet, a dead beloved

and the damned for company. Dogs follow and bare their teeth.
if I'm ready

Death borrows him. He listens to stones. His heart a coral labyrinth,
will go check

his mind on fire, his skin is warm.

waiting for an answer

let's discuss grasses

CHAPTER SIXTEEN: THE COMPLAINT

sunk, rudderless in a shallow pond, his mind churns and gives off sparks like some immense ironworks – sensation of Godhead encased in a scrawny carcass overwrought with raw thought spinning, consciousness as a contagious disease inflicting only oneself, shoaled, uncombed – weeds like sores, stars

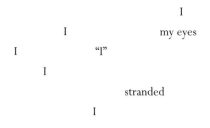

"the Complaint: if I shall exist eternally, then how shall I exist tomorrow?" does Spirit bark like a dog? prance through little wavelets at the Ostrava? does Immanence eat unleavened bread? how can the Soul bear to live as bone, muscle, blood, mucous, spittle, nausea, indecision, hi-jinks, time-wasting and pathetic snobberies about the style of a shoe or cravat? does the Absolute devour knackwürst with grainy mustard? when Pure Being gets cornered into a frail and finite selfhood, does it wave its insufficiency like a hanky into the winds of the Unknown?

CHAPTER SEVENTEEN: PASSAGE

*"I think we ought to read only the kind of books
that wound and stab us [beissen and stechen —
bite and cut]. We need books that affect us like
a disaster, that grieve us deeply ... like being
banished into the forests far from everyone, like
a suicide ... " [1903 letter to Franz Pollak]*

magnetized toward mantic foreboding and
inklings of hidden disease, a traveler sets out
toward some remote chance of recognition,
that sense that you were yourself in some way
a prefiguration of the passage, stream leading
to a small marl lake clotted with lily pads
streaked with blue dragonflies a passage that
now clarifies or at least reflects you unsteadily
in tremulous water that also contains sky and
smudgy willow branches pale-green with the
quiet, confident gestures of hands

like islands

that wax and wane

in this Untranslatable perhaps unknowable
place, given an utter lack of woodmanship
skills and a horizon which has receded taking
with it all sense of time and direction, perhaps
the only thing left for us to do now is lie down
together on the sandy ground and open our
hands toward the foreshortened expanse of
birch and pines populated with odd
unobtrusive noises, a reverberant illegible
speech that vibrates and hovers at a slight
distance from our bodies, no need to strain to
decipher this semiotics that appears to turn
away no one, not even wolves who approach
in unhurried, loping strides – whether their
echolalic *Sprechstimme* will compose the long-
desired lit fuse in leafy thicket: *"an axe breaking
into the frozen sea within us"* – is not yet
determined

whose mercy

falls

CHAPTER EIGHTEEN: IN A BEAUTIFUL LOCALITY

the day before his death, Kafka writes his parents
with heart-breaking jauntiness: *"I am still not very
pretty, [Ich bin noch immer nicht so schön] not a sight
worth seeing ... I mean to spend a few days together
peacefully in a beautiful locality. I don't remember when
the last time was ... 'having a good glass of beer together'
as you write ... when Father would take me along to the
public swimming pool"*

                            gone wholly into

        the bright, *gemütlich*

                              fractal

rubble

o swimmer, lie down in the full sweep of currents held in sleep of mineral

sway the city now a mirage eaten by green islands by willows and silt drift

is life more true in the fragmentary
drama of dreams where you reach
for a glass and your hand is not
actually your hand and it's very, very
important to finally reach your
destination which recedes, becoming
increasingly labyrinthine and hieratic
in impossibility, the empyrean cool
green and pleasant weather at the
beer garden, an Eden where you
swim in air like a trapeze-artist fish
and no net beneath you

                                                    wide-open

gears
                        sedimentary
                                        at the Crystal Palace

CHAPTER NINETEEN: OUR ANIMAL

"You can withdraw from the sufferings of the world —
that possibility is open to you and accords with your nature —
but perhaps that withdrawal is the only suffering you might
be able to avoid"[Zürau Notebook, No 103]

a small field creature you
are frantic with anxiety in
your burrow hearing an
unknown Enemy steadily
tunneling, tunneling toward
you and at this moment in
the entire universe is there

> shocked us from our absorption

anyone aside from a small,
fine-boned man who once
lived modestly in Prague
taking notice of your
imminent annihilation who
has chosen to share your
fate of gnawing and hiding
and cunning composed of
twigs and crumbled dirt?

CHAPTER TWENTY: AMPHIBIAN

skin fierce in its permeability, fore-runner, signal species

pay attention —

"I lay on the ground by the wall, writhing in pain, trying to burrow
into the damp earth"

a kind of castle or schloss looms and broods in the near-distance

guarded by sentries with rifles slung across thick uniforms

that resemble hair-pelts as they slouch in attitudes of sadistic ennui

ready for some sort of sport casting their casually indifferent

augenblick over the anguished new-comer

"The journey passed swiftly and smoothly; perishing of thirst, with open mouth
I breathed in the high swirling dust and now and then felt the gentleman's
delighted touch on my calves ..."

"really, don't trouble yourself" Our Animal tries to say placatingly

as cruel moonlight floods the scene like an interrogator

it seems to him that in this exam

no answers will ever be found acceptable

to the unspecified, gleefully menacing gentleman

standing in for the Terrifying Reader/Voyeur

perhaps you, *Hypocrite Lecteur*

as all-purpose, cross-century consumer that most resembles

one's own demographic or culinary profile

who, in another, more innocent age might think the ruins "gothic" "melancholy",

the character of the protagonist "masochistic"

"plaintive" "sentimental" "perverse" but we late-arrivals know the tale now falls more readily

into genres of documentary and what used to be known as science

drowned out by an avalanche of enticing

product placement inserted in regular intervals by part-time workers

into cheerfully reassuring

corporate tweets that fluff-dry yearning compounded

by general indifference or hopelessness

for we know of frogs born skinless and apocalyptic in wetlands

we speed past in marginally more or less fuel-efficient

vehicles while checking the latest number of comments

re-posting our earlier comments which

have been logo-rhythmically spread-sheeted

into chromographic intensities of the extent of one's market reach

and genetic viability at least

in the short-term

                              < mouth of dust, cast-off skin

CHAPTER TWENTY-ONE: READING

where every word is read as "*Jude*" every punctuation mark and margin

"*Jude*" "*Jude*" in every sky every thunderstorm the hailstones containing the hair of Jews

the streets and silences and stones — who will survive when it is whispered

that God was once a Jew but converted?

further into the dark conveyance beyond imagination

CHAPTER TWENTY-TWO: LIVE FEED

"put your hand on my forehead a moment to give me courage"—

necessity of touch, another kind of hunger

TANGLED BANK

LIVE FEED: standing in wild grasses

"It is interesting to contemplate a tangled bank, clothed with
　　　　　the distance from firestorm to paradiso
　　　　　　　　　　many plants
　　　　cool ultramarine surfaces　　　　within a hairsbreadth
of many kinds with birds singing on the bushes, with various
　　　　　　　　　　　　　　of your touch
　　　　insects flitting about and with worms crawling
　　　　　　"a strange vision is folding me into itself"
　　　　　　through the damp earth…"

IN AN ORCHARD, his back to us
mis-take assumes another take
Keats, soon to die, sits writing, entirely absorbed
is better, to commit the unkindness of wanting something else
like the blossoms themselves, full-warm
than what happened
in quickening spring, time is endless, children scour woods
generally, worms are not a mistake

they listen and listen

many things are found on the ground,

what you call "twig

with moss"   has never existed before

will never again, like this

_____

the Unwanted, twisted awkwardly   splinter of —

dangerous light, breathing

CHAPTER TWENTY-THREE: FEATHER

\# 44 *"a ridiculous way you have girded yourself for this world"*
\# 52 *"in the struggle between yourself and the world, hold the world's coat"*

prefiguring G——'s shabby Overcoat tossed on currents of Revolution,

flotsam of humanity, World Wars, treaties, forged and betrayed,

a single glossolalic crow feather buoyant on the spars and tumults

of fathomless flood-swollen rivers

feral nightfall
eiderdown, the unknown, ∧ burst into tears

shivved down like a knife

CHAPTER TWENTY-FOUR: THE WHOLE SKY

"Two possibilities: making oneself infinitely small or being so" [Zürau, No. 90]

one night after a long winter,
the window was thrown open to
the first lenience of Spring and
he awoke to find the bed
curtains shimmering with the
transcendental strobic inflor-
escence of fire-flies flickering
wildly, caught in folds of fabric
like a net of tenderness for
waves of tough little souls intent
on waking to their few minutes
of mortal life into a shine that
bites dog-like at our heels

spitting out
knit bios

CHAPTER TWENTY-FIVE: VEER

here comes a deer lifting its hooves

carefully across dry leaves then

another their heads raised, fleetness

implied in the stillness that attends

alluvial
    and attenuates their progress just as

morning opens its hands in the

meadow of deer, a goldfinch veers

attentive
    into yellow, you remind me of

goldfinches not so much their bright

swerve but how they interrupt

thought how they kill the idea of

gold or god or going or gone into

untraceable   shadow   protecting

grasses with their flight in the keep

of deer, oblique shifts of sight, the

lens whirring, you remind me of

goldfinches not their quickness and

yellow but their aptitude for dis-

"even in the

most secret emotions"

-appearance when morning opens
its hands the goldfinch is god flinch
a deer turns his head, grasses
knitted deep indigo, in this meadow
books live undomesticated in rank
hemlock sway, are we their neural
couriers their motion-forest are we

                                                               cast into
their   luck   their   fortune   their
nebulae are we the mirror of their
mirror gone out walking gone

the Open   through mud and marshy colluvium
the exact pivot where everything
can be healed past healing past the
anapestic flit-flit-flit of goldfinches
though we are never finally cured
from the affliction of their flight

                        their flood

                             unashamed

CHAPTER TWENTY-SIX: NARROW, WINDBLOWN

S O U L M A D E A P P A R E N T , visible by its absence —

a person, an animal, dusk or neighborhood, even a piece

of clothing instinctively knows when Soul has fled, is blank

buried, drowned, asleep or elsewhere,

if words cannot transform me, what can —

———————— W I L D E R N E S S

Unlanguaged sound within the words themselves?

———————————————

presence or absence of soul in a given moment

"we stand there, gazing down, stand at the edge

of a narrow, windblown . . ."

ACKNOWLEDGEMENTS

This work came into being when Kafka's biography and journals threaded themselves into my life spent with a welter of odd languages and people far from their homeland. His world seemed familiar/familial to me – my mother and her family fled Hungary after WWII; members of my father's family remained in Siberia, stranded for decades in labor camps.

There's both a covering and exposure of memory in rust, plant communities, the movement of geological and geo-political strata. History, like *Bios* (which famously "loves to hide"), appears to keep alive in stories that refuse to move in linear order, that both resist and desire revelation. It was after I finished this manuscript that I learned my mother had been an interpreter at Nuremberg, taking testimony from Goering and Horthy (the former Regent of Hungary). She just hadn't mentioned or uncovered it before.

These pages are inhabited by friends and other family who have moved through our successive living rooms in flux from Vienna, Italy, Dresden, Budapest, Sudetenland, Kazakhstan – leaving behind villages uprooted, families decimated, cities made unrecognizable, borders impossible to leave or enter – lives cast forth like "tough, mongrel" sema/seeds becoming transmitters of their own radically re-imagined words.

I owe everything to the resilience of their fragments of language and narrative, spoken and unspoken.

So many people are woven into the making of this book. I am grateful to the editors, curators and musicians who helped bring this work into a wider public realm:

GOD, in altered format, appeared in *The Volta*; lines from F ALLING UPRIGHT were used in "Tracing," a collaboration series with Denise Newman in VOL T. A portion of LIVE FEED appeared in *Mistake*, selected by Rosmarie Waldrop for the 2012 Caketrain chapbook competition, partly quoted from Darwin. Other lines from THE COMPLAINT also appeared in the altered book mixed-media series "The Queen Bee," a collaboration with painter Karen Ganz, originally in *HOW(ever)* as well as *translating the unspeakable: Poetry and the Innovative Necessity*, essays by Kathleen Fraser. In a previous version, the collection was a finalist for the Drunken Boat Hybrid Book Award; PASSAGE appears online in the Drunken Boat Hybrid Book Award folio, issue 21, along with a spoken version: http://www.drunkenboat.com/db21/book-contest-finalists/meredith-stricker. THE COMPLAINT, ELSEWHERE, VEER, and a section of WHY NOT IN THE FOREST appear in the online journal *opon*

This project began as a graphic-novel-poem where visual work was very much part its coming in being. I'm especially grateful for developing mixed-media used in this working process during the performance collaboration *"we are the bees of the invisible"* with musicians and composers Kumi Uyeda, Kallan Nishimoto, Mayaan Tsadka, Daniel Brown at Flytrap Studio in Oakland. A complete text of the performance appeared with a series of color projection stills in *webconjunctions* 02.12.14: http://www.conjunctions.com/webconj.htm

I am also deeply appreciative of support from:

intrepid collaborators in poetics, performance, visual work and narrative: Denise Newman, Lori Anderson Moseman, Kumi Uyeda, Israeli composer Mayaan Tsaka and her composition *Present Absentees*; András and Vera Nágy and family; Michelle Magdalena Maddox; for Canan Tolon's transformative visual work; Yong Soon Min and her exploration of the Korean diaspora; the radiant Laheys; everyone at Omnidawn for their tireless and inspired furthering of poetry; to Jodi McLean for compassionate support in the process of trauma recovery and a wider stream; my teacher, Okumura Roshi's translation work at the edge of language – and Thom Cowen, for continually opening the field

NOTES

additional credits:

visual elements are by the author, except for the photograph
of Franz Kafka as a university student, 1913: Jewish Chronicle
Archive, London / Art Resource, NY.

sources:

The Zürau Aphorisms of Franz Kafka, commentary by Roberto Calasso,
translated from the German by Michael Hoffman, Schocken Books

The Blue Octavo Notebooks, including *The Zürau Aphorisms as "Reflections on Sin,
Suffering, Hope and The True Way,"* Franz Kafka, edited by Max Brod, translated
by Ernst Kaiser and Eithne Wilkins, Exact Change, Cambridge

Franz Kafka, *Diaries 1910-1923*, edited by Max Brod, Schocken Books

Franz Kafka, "A Hunger Artist", "Metamorphosis", *Selected Short Stories of Franz
Kafka*; translated by Willa and Edwin Muir, Modern Library

Nicholas Murray, *Kafka: A Biography*, Yale University Press, 2004.
I am indebted to Nicholas Murray for his account of Kafka's death which is
lucidly and movingly told along with citations from the "conversation slips"
that Kafka used when it was no longer possible for him to speak.

Roberto Calasso, *K*

Gustaf Sobin, *Luminous Debris*, UC Berkeley Press

Preface: "why not in the forest ..." Kafka, *The Zürau Aphorisms*

Chapter one: "We were created..." Franz Kafka, *The Zürau Aphorisms of Franz Kafka*; Géza St. Galy, family friend, artist

Chapter three: "the delicate throat..." Franz Kafka, *Diaries 1910-1923*, edited by Max Brod, Schocken Books

Chapter four: quotations are from the previous chapter overlay text, "GOD"

Chapter six: "form shaped by the mobile"... Gustav Sobin, *Luminous Debris*, "certain images..." John Cage

Chapter seven: "Not until twilight..." Kafka, *Metamorphosis*; "in Hebrew my name ...", "perhaps only because..." Kafka, *Diaries 1910-1923*

Chapter nine: "how many years..." Franz Kafka, conversation slip, *Kafka: A Biography*, Nicholas Murray

"no employee..." policy of the Assicurazioni Generale Insurance Company where Kafka worked, quoted from *Kafka: A Biography*, Nicholas Murray

"beautiful hour...", Franz Kafka, quoted in *K*, Roberto Calasso, Knopf, 2004

Chapter ten: "Here, now..." Franz Kafka, conversation slip, *Kafka: A Biography*; "I couldn't find..." Franz Kafka, "A Hunger Artist," *Selected Short Stories of Franz Kafka*; translated by Willa and Edwin Muir, Modern Library

"SERAPHIC GENIUS", Walter Benjamin, *Walter Benjamin's Archive: Images, Texts, Signs*, 2007, edited by Ursula Marx, Gudrun Schwartz, Michael Schwartz, and Erdmut Wizisla

Chapter eleven: The name Kafka sounds like "kavka" or jackdaw (a European crow) in Czech; as Nicholas Murray writes, it is also "a reminder of the oppression of the Jews in the Hapsburg Empire", where the use of Hebrew and Yiddish was banned for official records and Jews were made to "abandon their Jewish patronymics and adopt German personal and family names."

Chapter twelve: "How we used to undress…" Kafka recounting the story of the swimming pool and his father to Dora, *Kafka: A Biography*, Nicholas Murray

"poplar whirled out…" Franz Kafka, *Diaries 1910-1923*, edited by Max Brod, Schocken Books

Chapter fourteen: "Bed, constipation…", "looking at myself…" Kafka, *Blue Octavo Notebooks*

Chapter fifteen: "December 22…", "January 17…", "January 22…" Kafka, *Blue Octavo Notebooks*; "selvaggio e aspro e fort" (wild and rough and stubborn): Dante, *The Inferno*

Chapter sixteen: "the complaint…" Kafka, *Blue Octavo Notebooks*

Chapter seventeen: "I think we ought to read …", Kafka letter to Franz Pollak, 1903; "An axe breaking into…", Ibid.

Chapter eighteen: "I am still not …", Franz Kafka, letter to his parents while at the clinic, *Kafka: A Biography*, Nicholas Murray

Chapter nineteen: I first came across this photograph of Kafka and an Alsation in Jean-Christophe Bailly's *The Animal Side (Le versant animal)*. Bailly speaks of Kafka as *"the only writer who has given animals speech … and succeeded in doing so in a register that was no longer that of the fable … in Kafka's texts animals seem to be resurfacing from some obscure depths, as it were, and appropriating human language for themselves in order to shed light on those depths. With small rodents in particular, there is almost something like a transference, involving a whole set of infinitesimal notations of sound and touch …"*

"a small field creature" echoes back to Kafka's story "The Burrow"

Chapter twenty: "I lay on the ground …", "the journey passed…." Kafka, *Blue Octavo Notebooks*

Chapter twenty-two: "Put your hand…" Franz Kafka, conversation slip, *Kafka: A Biography*, Nicholas Murray; "it is interesting…": Darwin, *The Origin of Species*; "a strange vision is …": Dante, *The Inferno*

Chapter twenty-three: "a ridiculous way ..."; "in the struggle..." Kafka, *The Zürau Aphorisms*; "G—'s overcoat", refers to Gogol's story and its affinities with Kafka, also Beckett's G—

Chapter twenty-four: "Two possibilities..." *The Zürau Aphorisms as "Reflections on Sin, Suffering, Hope and The True Way"*

shiv: knife, from Romany *chiv*: an echo of shiver and slivers of broken glass fragments

Chapter twenty-five: "even in the most secret...": Franz Kafka, *Diaries 1910-1923*, edited by Max Brod, Schocken Books

Chapter twenty-six: "we stand there, gazing down..." Gustaf Sobin, *Luminous Debris*, UC Berkeley Press

Meredith Stricker is an artist, designer and poet who has published three collections of poetry involving performance, graphic overlays and hybrid forms of documentary/lyric. She is co-director of <u>visual poetry collaborative</u> focusing on architecture in Big Sur and projects to bring together artists, writers, musicians and experimental media. Her poetry and visual work have appeared widely in journals as well as in galleries, museums and performance spaces.

Our Animal by Meredith Stricker

Cover and interior text set in Trajan Pro,
Abadi MT Condensed Extra Bold, and Perpetua Std

Cover art © Canan Tolon
Untitled, 1996; acrylic, oil and rust on linen; 76 X 61 cm / 30 X 24 inches

Photo of Franz Kafka on page 53 © HIP / Art Resource, NY
Franz Kafka (1883-1924), Czech writer, as a university student, 1913.
Jewish Chronicle Archive

Cover and interior design by Gillian Olivia Blythe Hamel

Offset printed in the United States
by Edwards Brothers Malloy, Ann Arbor, Michigan
On 55# Heritage Book Cream White Antique

Omnidawn Publishing
Richmond, California
2016

Rusty Morrison & Ken Keegan, senior editors & co-publishers
Gillian Olivia Blythe Hamel, managing editor
Melissa Burke, marketing manager
Cassandra Smith, poetry editor & book designer
Peter Burghardt, poetry editor & book designer
Sharon Zetter, poetry editor, book designer & development officer
Liza Flum, poetry editor & marketing assistant
Juliana Paslay, fiction editor
Gail Aronson, fiction editor
RJ Ingram, *OmniVerse* contributing editor
Kevin Peters, marketing assistant & *OmniVerse* Lit Scene editor
Trisha Peck, marketing assistant
Sara Burant, administrative assistant
Josie Gallup, publicity assistant
SD Sumner, publicity assistant

Publication of this book was made possible in part by gifts from:
Robin & Curt Caton
John Gravendyk